The Writer's Thoughts

THIS JOURNAL BELONGS TO

The Writer's Journal is a product of Mythical Legends Publishing
ISBN: **978-1-943958-98-6**
Copyright © 2018 by Mythical Legends Publishing
First Edition Published 2018

987654321

The Writer's Thoughts

Breathe. Exhale. Write.

noun
    a person who commits his or her thoughts, ideas, etc., to writing.

Table of Contents

Common Fiction Genres	5
Loglines	8
Common Archetypes	9
Story Thoughts	10
Whiteboard	50
Notes	82
Character Sketch	114
World Sketch	154

"If you can tell stories, create characters, devise incidents, and have sincerity and passion, it doesn't matter a damn how you write."
- Somerset Maugham

I have been successful probably because I have always realized that I knew nothing about writing and have merely tried to tell an interesting story entertainingly."
- Edgar Rice Burroughs

COMMON FICTION GENRES

Classic
fiction that has become part of an accepted literary canon, widely taught in schools

Comics/Graphic novel
comic magazine or book based on a sequence of pictures (often hand drawn) and few words.

Crime/detective
fiction about a crime, how the criminal gets caught, and the repercussions of the crime

Fable
legendary, supernatural tale demonstrating a useful truth

Fairy tale
story about fairies or other magical creatures

Fan fiction
fiction written by a fan of, and featuring characters from, a particular TV series, movie, or book. Usually takes place on platforms, such as Fanfiction.net or Wattpad

Fantasy
fiction in a unreal setting that often includes magic, magical creatures, or the supernatural

Folklore
the songs, stories, myths, and proverbs of a people or "folk" as handed down by word of mouth

Historical fiction
story with fictional characters and events in an historical setting

Horror
fiction in which events evoke a feeling of dread and sometimes fear in both the characters and the reader

Humor
usually a fiction full of fun, fancy, and excitement, meant to entertain and sometimes cause intended laughter; but can be contained in all genres

Legend
story, sometimes of a national or folk hero, that has a basis in fact but also includes imaginative material

Magical realism
story where magical or unreal elements play a natural part in an otherwise realistic environment

Meta fiction *(also known as romantic irony in the context of Romantic works of literature)*
uses self-reference to draw attention to itself as a work of art while exposing the "truth" of a story

Mystery
fiction dealing with the solution of a crime or the revealing of secrets

Mythology
legend or traditional narrative, often based in part on historical events, that reveals human behavior and natural phenomena by its symbolism; often pertaining to the actions of the gods

Mythopoeia
fiction in which characters from religious mythology, traditional myths, folklore and/or history are recast into a re-imagined realm created by the author

Picture book
picture storybook is a book with very little words and a lot of pictures; picture stories are usually for children

Realistic fiction
story that is true to life

Science fiction
story based on the impact of actual, imagined, or potential science, often set in the future or on other planets

Short story
fiction of great brevity, usually supports no subplots

Suspense/thriller
fiction about harm about to befall a person or group and the attempts made to evade the harm

Tall tale
humorous story with blatant exaggerations, such as swaggering heroes who do the impossible with nonchalance

Western
fiction set in the American Old West frontier and typically in the late eighteenth to late nineteenth century

SOURCE
https://en.wikipedia.org/wiki/List_of_writing_genres

Loglines

Below is the Killogator logline formula and steps to creating a killer logline:

The first thing to do is write out the WHO, WHAT, WHERE, WHEN, and WHY. Graeme Shimmin, Writing a Killer Logline, outlines six items:

SETTING: When and where does the story takes place.
PROTAGONIST: Who is the main character?
PROBLEM: The issue or event that causes the Protagonist to take action.
ANTAGONIST: Who or what tries to stop the Protagonist.
CONFLICT: The major obstacle, difficulty or dilemma the protagonist faces.
GOAL: What the Protagonist hopes to win, achieve, find or defeat.

Here is the formula:

In a (**SETTING**) a (**PROTAGONIST**) has a (**PROBLEM**) (caused by an **ANTAGONIST**) and (faces **CONFLICT**) as they try to (achieve a **GOAL**).

For more insightful information on creating great loglines, please visit Graeme Shimmin's wedsite: **Writing a Killer Logline:**
http://graemeshimmin.com/writing-a-logline-for-a-novel/

COMMON ARCHETYPES

Hero
The hero is the audience's personal tour guide on the adventure that is the story.

Mentor
The hero has to learn how to survive in the new world incredibly fast, so the mentor appears to give them a fighting chance.

Ally
The hero will have some great challenges ahead; too great for one person to face them alone.

Herald
The herald appears near the beginning to announce the need for change in the hero's life.

Trickster
The trickster adds fun and humor to the story.

Shapeshifter
The shapeshifter blurs the line between ally and enemy.

Guardian
The guardian, or threshold guardian, tests the hero before they face great challenges.

Shadow
The Villians of the story

SOURCE:
https://mythcreants.com/blog/the-eight-character-archetypes-of-the-heros-journey/

STORY THOUGHTS

Working Title:

Final Title:

Genre:
Author's Name:

Logline:

Story Summary:

Plot ideas:

Scene ideas:

Continued

Scene ideas:

Notes:

STORY THOUGHTS

Working Title:

Final Title:

Genre:
Author's Name:

Logline:

Story Summary:

Plot ideas:

Scene ideas:

Continued

Scene ideas:

Notes:

STORY THOUGHTS

Working Title:

Final Title:

Genre:

Author's Name:

Logline:

Story Summary:

Plot ideas:

Scene ideas:

Continued

Scene ideas:

Notes:

STORY THOUGHTS

Working Title:

Final Title:

Genre:

Author's Name:

Logline:

Story Summary:

Plot ideas:

Scene ideas:

Continued

Scene ideas:

Notes:

STORY THOUGHTS

Working Title:

Final Title:

Genre:
Author's Name:

Logline:

Story Summary:

Plot ideas:

Scene ideas:

Continued

Scene ideas:

Notes:

STORY THOUGHTS

Working Title:

Final Title:

Genre:

Author's Name:

Logline:

Story Summary:

Plot ideas:

Scene ideas:

Continued

Scene ideas:

Notes:

STORY THOUGHTS

Working Title:

Final Title:

Genre:
Author's Name:

Logline:

Story Summary:

Plot ideas:

Scene ideas:

Scene ideas: _____ Continued

Notes:

STORY THOUGHTS

Working Title:

Final Title:

Genre:
Author's Name:

Logline:

Story Summary:

Plot ideas:

Scene ideas:

Continued

Scene ideas:

Notes:

STORY THOUGHTS

Working Title:

Final Title:

Genre:

Author's Name:

Logline:

Story Summary:

Plot ideas:

Scene ideas:

Continued

Scene ideas:

Notes:

STORY THOUGHTS

Working Title:

Final Title:

Genre:
Author's Name:

Logline:

Story Summary:

Plot ideas:

Scene ideas:

Continued

Scene ideas:

Notes:

WHITEBOARD

WHITEBOARD

WHITEBOARD

WHITEBOARD

WHITEBOARD

WHITEBOARD

WHITEBOARD

WHITEBOARD

WHITEBOARD

WHITEBOARD

WHITEBOARD

WHITEBOARD

WHITEBOARD

WHITEBOARD

WHITEBOARD

WHITEBOARD

NOTES

NOTES

NOTES

NOTES

NOTES

NOTES

NOTES

NOTES

NOTES

NOTES

NOTES

NOTES

NOTES

NOTES

NOTES

NOTES

CHARACTER SKETCH

Character Name:

Age:

Transgender: YES/NO

Female   Male

Height:

Weight:

Eye Color:

Hair Color:

Skin Color:

Nationality/Ethnicity:

Religion/Belief:

Current Occupation:

Education:

History/Backstory:

Quick Notes:

CHARACTER SKETCH

Character Name:

Age:

Transgender: YES/NO
Female   Male

Height:

Weight:

Eye Color:

Hair Color:

Skin Color:

Nationality/Ethnicity:

Religion/Belief:

Current Occupation:

Education:

History/Backstory:

Quick Notes:

CHARACTER SKETCH

Character Name:

Age:

Transgender: YES/NO
Female   Male

Height:

Weight:

Eye Color:

Hair Color:

Skin Color:

Nationality/Ethnicity:

Religion/Belief:

Current Occupation:

Education:

History/Backstory:

Quick Notes:

CHARACTER SKETCH

Character Name:

Age:

Transgender: YES/NO

Female   Male

Height:

Weight:

Eye Color:

Hair Color:

Skin Color:

Nationality/Ethnicity:

Religion/Belief:

Current Occupation:

Education:

History/Backstory:

Quick Notes:

CHARACTER SKETCH

Character Name:

Age:

Transgender: YES/NO
Female   Male

Height:

Weight:

Eye Color:

Hair Color:

Skin Color:

Nationality/Ethnicity:

Religion/Belief:

Current Occupation:

Education:

History/Backstory:

Quick Notes:

CHARACTER SKETCH

Character Name:

Age:

Transgender: YES/NO

Female   Male

Height:

Weight:

Eye Color:

Hair Color:

Skin Color:

Nationality/Ethnicity:

Religion/Belief:

Current Occupation:

Education:

History/Backstory:

Quick Notes:

CHARACTER SKETCH

Character Name:

Age:

Transgender: YES/NO

Female   Male

Height:

Weight:

Eye Color:

Hair Color:

Skin Color:

Nationality/Ethnicity:

Religion/Belief:

Current Occupation:

Education:

History/Backstory:

Quick Notes:

CHARACTER SKETCH

Character Name:

Age:

Transgender: YES/NO
Female   Male

Height:

Weight:

Eye Color:

Hair Color:

Skin Color:

Nationality/Ethnicity:

Religion/Belief:

Current Occupation:

Education:

History/Backstory:

Quick Notes:

CHARACTER SKETCH

Character Name:

Age:

Transgender: YES/NO

Female   Male

Height:

Weight:

Eye Color:

Hair Color:

Skin Color:

Nationality/Ethnicity:

Religion/Belief:

Current Occupation:

Education:

History/Backstory:

Quick Notes:

CHARACTER SKETCH

Character Name:

Age:

Transgender: YES/NO

Female　　　Male

Height:

Weight:

Eye Color:

Hair Color:

Skin Color:

Nationality/Ethnicity:

Religion/Belief:

Current Occupation:

Education:

History/Backstory:

Quick Notes:

CHARACTER SKETCH

Character Name:

Age:

Transgender: YES/NO

Female   Male

Height:

Weight:

Eye Color:

Hair Color:

Skin Color:

Nationality/Ethnicity:

Religion/Belief:

Current Occupation:

Education:

History/Backstory:

Quick Notes:

CHARACTER SKETCH

Character Name:

Age:

Transgender: YES/NO
Female   Male

Height:

Weight:

Eye Color:

Hair Color:

Skin Color:

Nationality/Ethnicity:

Religion/Belief:

Current Occupation:

Education:

History/Backstory:

Quick Notes:

CHARACTER SKETCH

Character Name:

Age:

Transgender: YES/NO

Female   Male

Height:

Weight:

Eye Color:

Hair Color:

Skin Color:

Nationality/Ethnicity:

Religion/Belief:

Current Occupation:

Education:

History/Backstory:

Quick Notes:

CHARACTER SKETCH

Character Name:

Age:

Transgender: YES/NO
Female   Male

Height:

Weight:

Eye Color:

Hair Color:

Skin Color:

Nationality/Ethnicity:

Religion/Belief:

Current Occupation:

Education:

History/Backstory:

Quick Notes:

CHARACTER SKETCH

Character Name:

Age:

Transgender: YES/NO
Female   Male

Height:

Weight:

Eye Color:

Hair Color:

Skin Color:

Nationality/Ethnicity:

Religion/Belief:

Current Occupation:

Education:

History/Backstory:

Quick Notes:

CHARACTER SKETCH

Character Name:

Age:

Transgender: YES/NO

Female   Male

Height:

Weight:

Eye Color:

Hair Color:

Skin Color:

Nationality/Ethnicity:

Religion/Belief:

Current Occupation:

Education:

History/Backstory:

Quick Notes:

CHARACTER SKETCH

Character Name:

Age:

Transgender: YES/NO

Female   Male

Height:

Weight:

Eye Color:

Hair Color:

Skin Color:

Nationality/Ethnicity:

Religion/Belief:

Current Occupation:

Education:

History/Backstory:

Quick Notes:

CHARACTER SKETCH

Character Name:

Age:

Transgender: YES/NO

Female   Male

Height:

Weight:

Eye Color:

Hair Color:

Skin Color:

Nationality/Ethnicity:

Religion/Belief:

Current Occupation:

Education:

History/Backstory:

Quick Notes:

CHARACTER SKETCH

Character Name:

Age:

Transgender: YES/NO
Female   Male

Height:

Weight:

Eye Color:

Hair Color:

Skin Color:

Nationality/Ethnicity:

Religion/Belief:

Current Occupation:

Education:

History/Backstory:

Quick Notes:

CHARACTER SKETCH

Character Name:

Age:

Transgender: YES/NO
Female   Male

Height:

Weight:

Eye Color:

Hair Color:

Skin Color:

Nationality/Ethnicity:

Religion/Belief:

Current Occupation:

Education:

History/Backstory:

Quick Notes:

WORLD SKETCH

Place Name:

Time period:

Area Description:

Governing body:

Politics:

Religion/Beliefs:

Population:

Competing/Rival/Hostile Neighbor:

Economics:

Dangers:

Notes:

WORLD SKETCH

Place Name:

Time period:

Area Description:

Governing body:

Politics:

Religion/Beliefs:

Population:

Competing/Rival/Hostile Neighbor:

Economics:

Dangers:

Notes:

WORLD SKETCH

Place Name:

Time period:

Area Description:

Governing body:

Politics:

Religion/Beliefs:

Population:

Competing/Rival/Hostile Neighbor:

Economics:

Dangers:

Notes:

WORLD SKETCH

Place Name:

Time period:

Area Description:

Governing body:

Politics:

Religion/Beliefs:

Population:

Competing/Rival/Hostile Neighbor:

Economics:

Dangers:

Notes:

WORLD SKETCH

Place Name:

Time period:

Area Description:

Governing body:

Politics:

Religion/Beliefs:

Population:

Competing/Rival/Hostile Neighbor:

Economics:

Dangers:

Notes:

WORLD SKETCH

Place Name:

Time period:

Area Description:

Governing body:

Politics:

Religion/Beliefs:

Population:

Competing/Rival/Hostile Neighbor:

Economics:

Dangers:

Notes:

WORLD SKETCH

Place Name:

Time period:

Area Description:

Governing body:

Politics:

Religion/Beliefs:

Population:

Competing/Rival/Hostile Neighbor:

Economics:

Dangers:

Notes:

WORLD SKETCH

Place Name:

Time period:

Area Description:

Governing body:

Politics:

Religion/Beliefs:

Population:

Competing/Rival/Hostile Neighbor:

Economics:

Dangers:

Notes:

WORLD SKETCH

Place Name:

Time period:

Area Description:

Governing body:

Politics:

Religion/Beliefs:

Population:

Competing/Rival/Hostile Neighbor:

Economics:

Dangers:

Notes:

WORLD SKETCH

Place Name:

Time period:

Area Description:

Governing body:

Politics:

Religion/Beliefs:

Population:

Competing/Rival/Hostile Neighbor:

Economics:

Dangers:

Notes:

WORLD SKETCH

Place Name:

Time period:

Area Description:

Governing body:

Politics:

Religion/Beliefs:

Population:

Competing/Rival/Hostile Neighbor:

Economics:

Dangers:

Notes:

www.ingramcontent.com/pod-product-compliance
Lightning Source LLC
Chambersburg PA
CBHW071615080526
44588CB00010B/1142